The TRUE STORY of VANILLA

HOW EDMOND ALBIUS MADE HISTORY

ANN RICHARDS

illustrated by
ARDEN TAYLOR

ORCA biography

ORCA BOOK PUBLISHERS

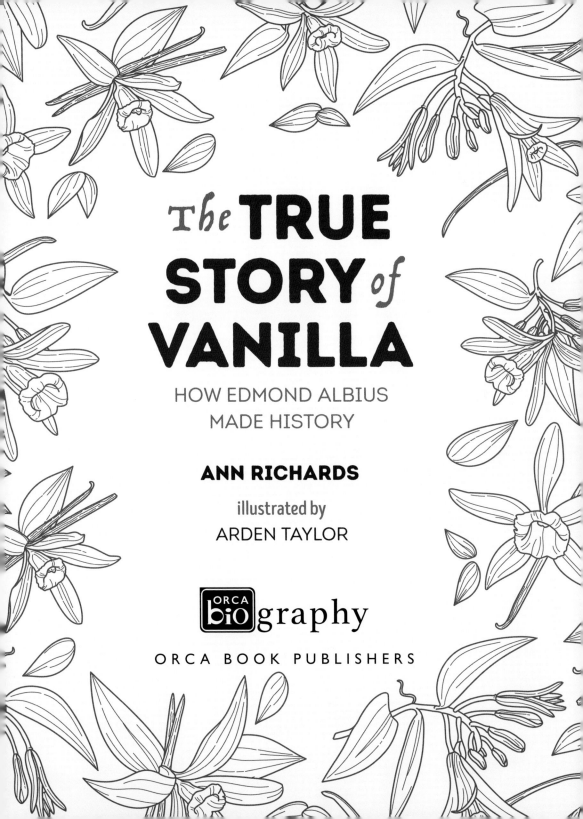

To my love…my sweet mommy, who helped me write this book. We finished on time.

Text copyright © Ann Richards 2025
Illustrations copyright © Arden Taylor 2025

Published in Canada and the United States in 2025 by Orca Book Publishers.
orcabook.com

All rights are reserved, including those for text and data mining, AI training and similar technologies. No part of this publication may be reproduced or transmitted in any form or by any means, electronic or mechanical, including photocopying, recording or by any information storage and retrieval system now known or to be invented, without permission in writing from the publisher. The publisher expressly prohibits the use of this work in connection with the development of any software program, including, without limitation, training a machine-learning or generative artificial intelligence (AI) system.

Library and Archives Canada Cataloguing in Publication

Title: The true story of vanilla : how Edmond Albius made history / Ann Richards ; illustrated by Arden Taylor.
Names: Richards, Ann (Ann M.), author. | Taylor, Arden, illustrator.
Description: Series statement: Orca biography ; 3 | Includes bibliographical references and index.
Identifiers: Canadiana (print) 20240418654 | Canadiana (ebook) 20240418662 | ISBN 9781459838444 (hardcover) | ISBN 9781459838451 (PDF) | ISBN 9781459838468 (EPUB)
Subjects: LCSH: Albius, Edmond, 1829-1880—Juvenile literature. | LCSH: Enslaved children—Réunion—Biography—Juvenile literature. | LCSH: Vanilla—Pollination—History—Juvenile literature. | LCGFT: Biographies. | LCGFT: Informational works.
Classification: LCC HD9212.5.V342 R53 2025 | DDC j338.1/7382092—dc23

Library of Congress Control Number: 2024938992

Summary: Part of the Orca Biography series for middle-grade readers, this illustrated nonfiction book tells the story of how an enslaved boy, Edmond Albius, discovered how to hand-pollinate vanilla, a technique that is still used all over the world today.

Orca Book Publishers is committed to reducing the consumption of nonrenewable resources in the production of our books. We make every effort to use materials that support a sustainable future.

Orca Book Publishers gratefully acknowledges the support for its publishing programs provided by the following agencies: the Government of Canada, the Canada Council for the Arts and the Province of British Columbia through the BC Arts Council and the Book Publishing Tax Credit.

The author and publisher have made every effort to ensure that the information in this book was correct at the time of publication. The author and publisher do not assume any liability for any loss, damage, or disruption caused by errors or omissions. Every effort has been made to trace copyright holders and to obtain their permission for the use of copyrighted material. The publisher apologizes for any errors or omissions and would be grateful if notified of any corrections that should be incorporated in future reprints or editions of this book.

Cover and interior artwork by Arden Taylor.
Design by Troy Cunningham.
Edited by Kirstie Hudson.

Printed and bound in South Korea.

28 27 26 25 • 1 2 3 4

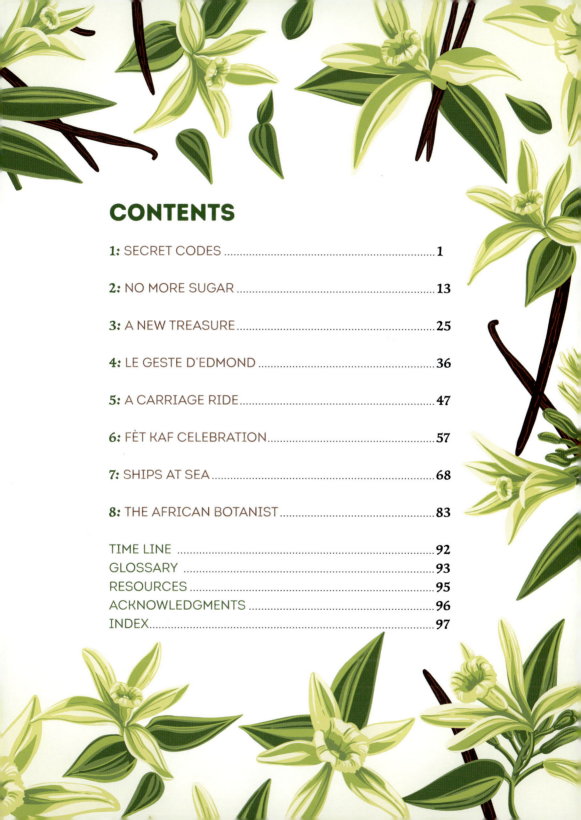

CONTENTS

1: SECRET CODES 1

2: NO MORE SUGAR 13

3: A NEW TREASURE 25

4: LE GESTE D'EDMOND 36

5: A CARRIAGE RIDE 47

6: FÈT KAF CELEBRATION 57

7: SHIPS AT SEA 68

8: THE AFRICAN BOTANIST 83

TIME LINE 92
GLOSSARY 93
RESOURCES 95
ACKNOWLEDGMENTS 96
INDEX 97

His name was Edmond, and he was born in August, 1829, on the Bellier-Beaumont sugar **plantation** in Sainte-Suzanne, on a small island in the Indian Ocean called Réunion. Edmond's parents were both **slaves**, owned by Elvire Bellier-Beaumont, and like others **enslaved** in French colonies, they were not allowed to keep their own surnames or possess anything, even shoes, and they never received payment for all their hard work. His mother, Mélise, was a maid. She died at age 28, giving birth to Edmond. He never knew his father, Pamphile, who died when Edmond was about 19.

A PLACE *for a* HOUSEBOY

Elvire cared for Edmond when he was a baby and a small child. She later sent Edmond to live with her brother, a childless widower named Ferréol Bellier-Beaumont, to work as a **houseboy** on his sugar plantation just a few miles away. The Réunion **census** shows that Edmond arrived at the Bellevue plantation sometime in 1834, when he was five years old. He is described as "Black, with wooly hair." Ferréol was not rich like other plantation owners on Réunion, but his plantation was similar to others on the island and around the world.

SECRET CODES

Plantations typically had a large main house with lots of rooms, each decorated with nice furniture for the **master** and his family. Slaves' houses were very different. The slaves made them themselves, using palm leaves, sugarcane straw, tree trunks, branches and clay, or they were built from worn wooden slats, leftover materials from the master's house, that were nailed together. They didn't have beds, so they slept on the floor, using hay or dry grass as mattresses.

Most plantations had a flower and vegetable garden, and they grew coffee and, later, sugarcane, which were the main crops on Réunion. Slaves planted and harvested sugarcane in hot sun. They spent hours with machetes, chopping the stalks of cane and then tying them into tall bundles before carrying them on their backs to the sugar mill. The slaves had to work very hard for their masters.

Many slaves escaped from their plantations. The slaves wanted to be free and return to the countries they had been stolen from. Brave slaves carved boats out of trees, hoping to get away in the dark of night and row across the sea to Madagascar, Comoros or Africa. Some made it home, but others died on the journey.

Life was very different for Edmond. He lived with his master, Ferréol, in the main house. It was unusual for the children of slaves to live with their master. Countries such as the United States, England, Portugal, Spain and France had laws for the treatment of slaves. But unlike Réunion's other French **colonizers**,

LE CODE NOIR (THE BLACK CODE)
The Code Noir was written by the French government in 1685. The code had 60 articles that controlled the lives, deaths, purchases, punishments and cultural and religious beliefs of slaves. It dictated how masters in all French colonies should treat their slaves. It was created to ensure that slaves remained obedient and to prevent revolts.

Ferréol did not follow the **Code Noir** (Black Code), the French laws that instructed masters on how to treat slaves (known as **noirs de pioche**, or pickax blacks).

A CHILD *in the* GARDEN

Ferréol, a **Creole**, was born on the island and was a well-known **botanist** in the community. He enjoyed experimenting with rare plants. Edmond spent most of his days with Ferréol, walking around the plantation and the garden. Ferréol taught Edmond everything he knew about the various trees and plants on the plantation during these daily walks. Edmond enjoyed studying plants, observing their changes from seed to sprout and finally

flowering. He learned about the importance of bees.

Ferréol's friends, other plantation owners and other slaves noticed that Edmond was a smart child. Edmond's interest in **botany** and his ability to understand science created a unique relationship between him and his master. "That little black Creole, a slave of my sister's, was my favorite and constantly at my side," Ferréol wrote in a letter years later.

While it has been suggested that some slave owners treated enslaved people with a degree of decency relative to the harsh norms of the time, we must never forget that the institution of slavery is unjust and inhumane. Any perceived kindness does not negate the violation of freedom, dignity and human rights that slavery represents.

FLOWERS PRODUCE FOOD

Ferréol had many trees and plants. His favorite was a rare white vanilla plant that climbed a pole in the garden. Its leaves were flat and the vine grew to a height of nearly 50 feet (15 meters). He'd received vanilla cuttings that had been brought to Réunion from the Jardin des Plantes (Botanical Gardens) in Paris, and this was the only plant that had survived. But it never produced fruit, only white flowers during spring. Every season he watched and waited for vanilla fruit to appear, but nothing happened. Neither the birds nor the bees helped pollinate his rare plant. Ferréol voiced his frustration each time he and Edmond walked through the garden.

Ferréol wanted to start a new industry on Réunion, but although there were some 100 vanilla orchids growing on the island, they never bore fruit. Everyone around the world wanted vanilla to flavor their favorite foods, mix with chocolate or use for medicine. But at that time, the vanilla fruit was found only in Mexico because the bees there seemed to be the only ones that could pollinate the plant. This made vanilla a rare and expensive spice. Ferréol explained to Edmond that for more than 300 years, botanists all around the world had been trying to figure out how to pollinate the vanilla flower and had so far failed.

Botanists Joseph Henri Neumann from France and Charles François Morren from Belgium grew vanilla plants in a greenhouse and were the first to discover how the **Melipona** bee,

a stingless bee in Mexico, pollinated the flower. But, like Ferréol's, neither Neumann's nor Morren's own plants ever produced long green vanilla pods. Ferréol's frustration grew, but he continued to teach Edmond about the science of plants. And Edmond followed the honeybees and studied the flowers while the other slaves worked.

THE HISTORY *of* RÉUNION

Arab, Portuguese, Dutch and French sailors explored the island, but it remained uninhabited until the mid-1600s, when French colonizers arrived. Louis XIII had named the island Bourbon in 1649, after the French Royal House of Bourbon. In 1664 France and India formed the French East India Company to trade goods. With the need for a workforce, the colonizers soon began capturing people from Africa, Madagascar and India, bringing them back in **coffles** for agricultural work and domestic services on the island and in neighboring countries. The name was changed to Réunion in 1793, during the French Revolution. For a short time, starting in 1806, it was known as Bonaparte Island in honor of Napoleon Bonaparte, who had become the French

MARIE ANNE THÉRÈSE OMBLINE DESBASSAYNS (1755-1846)

Marie Anne Thérèse Ombline Desbassayns followed the Code Noir. History says she ruled over her plantation with an iron fist. She was forced to build a hospital because she had one of the largest plantations, with more than 460 slaves. Her slaves picked cotton, coffee and cloves and chopped sugarcane for the sugar mill. At midnight Madame Desbassayns sent the slaves to La Glacière, a cave deep in the mountains, to collect ice to sell to hospitals and slave ships or to cool her drinks or make ice cream. The slaves were not allowed to let the ice melt, so they had to return with it by sunrise.

emperor in 1804. In 1810 the island was known as Bourbon again. In 1811 more than 200 slaves—**overseers**, field workers, blacksmiths and house servants—revolted against their masters and lost. Finally, on December 20, 1848, France abolished the slave trade, but the practice of using **indentured workers** remained. That year the island's name changed yet again, reverting to Réunion, and this time the name stuck.

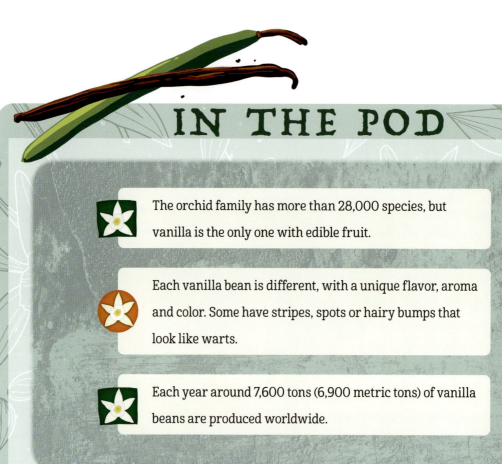

IN THE POD

- The orchid family has more than 28,000 species, but vanilla is the only one with edible fruit.

- Each vanilla bean is different, with a unique flavor, aroma and color. Some have stripes, spots or hairy bumps that look like warts.

- Each year around 7,600 tons (6,900 metric tons) of vanilla beans are produced worldwide.

SECRET CODES

- Vanilla is the world's most popular scent and flavor.
- The vanilla flower blooms for just a few hours, and it has underground and aerial roots.
- Spiders don't like vanilla.
- A cured vanilla bean left open works as an air freshener.

ANN RICHARDS

Edmond's birthplace, the small town of Sainte-Suzanne, was near the Manuel and LaVigne ravines, known as the sugarcane cradle. The 1820 census records the Bellier-Beaumont and Bellevue plantations as two of the first 10 estates to grow sugarcane. Years earlier four cyclones had destroyed the coffee and clove industries, so Réunion needed a new agricultural product. The Bellier-Beaumont plantation had 37 slaves who harvested the cane, managed the **sugar press** and the **still**, and manufactured rum. The Bellevue plantation also grew cane for the family and for local businesses and had as many as 50 slaves—Creoles, Africans, Madagascans and East Indians. With competition from the industries in Cuba and Europe, cane growers on Réunion concluded it would no longer be profitable to produce cane, so most of the slaves at the two plantations were sold to other plantations. However, Ferréol continued to grow a small amount of cane for a local company. He also grew other products, including figs, pumpkins, bananas, pineapples, tomatoes and sweet potatoes. His once busy plantation went down to six domestic slaves. The plantations needed a new product.

A SPECIAL CHILD

Ferréol considered Edmond a special child. Ferréol's best friend, Auguste Mézières-Lépervanche, Sainte-Suzanne's justice of the peace, said in a letter that Edmond was a spoiled child, treated "more as a son than as his slave." Edmond lived as a free person on the Bellevue plantation, playing in the gardens. He never worked in the fields or the house. Edmond never became a houseboy like his friends, the other slaves on the plantation. Instead, Ferréol's ambitions became Edmond's aspirations. Edmond grew up in the company of lawyers, politicians, plantation owners and other scientists and naturalists who visited the plantation. In a few years, these same men would ask Edmond for his help, and this would take Edmond and Ferréol on an amazing journey.

THE LITTLEST BOTANIST

It was sometime in 1835, not long after Edmond arrived at the Bellevue plantation, that he took the first of what were to become daily walks with Ferréol. The morning sun was often hot, and the ocean breeze would brush across the tops of the slaves' straw homes, blowing through the drying sheds and whistling over the sparse fields of thick cane grass.

Edmond and Ferréol started each morning walk side by side in the garden. Ferréol specialized in the study of rare agricultural crops—his garden was his life's work. As Edmond grew up, he was always listening, learning and imitating his master. Edmond analyzed the blossoming fields of purple, orange and yellow flowers, identifying male and female plants—the kind of microscopic details that are the first step in the study of plant life. Young Edmond spoke only Creole, didn't know the alphabet and didn't go to school, but Ferréol wanted him to learn. Soon

Edmond could describe all the plants and trees using the scientific language of the famous botanists Carl Linnaeus and Antoine Laurent de Jussieu. He knew Ferréol's rare vanilla plant was called *Vanilla planifolia*, that it was an **ephemeral** plant and that it grew fruit only in Mexico.

THE BUZZ *about* BEES

Plants are pollinated primarily by bees, but most can be pollinated by hand if practicality is not an issue. Ferréol wanted to boost his crops and help the bees, so he decided to try pollinating his pumpkin plants by hand. Pumpkin flowers open early in

A BIG JOB FOR A BEE

Melipona beecheii is a stingless bee native only to Mexico. It can pollinate the vanilla orchid because it has a longer snout than other pollinating insects. This harmless bee helps in the production of food by pollinating the plants in its ecosystem. Maya people in Mexico have kept these bees for producing *Melipona* honey for over 3,000 years. The honey, which is slightly sour and very nutritious, is used as medicine for the ears and eyes and to help with colds and digestive problems. Maya people protect this bee. They call it *Xunan kab*, which means "the royal lady."

the morning and close early. Hand-pollinating needs to be done before 10 a.m. Ferréol examined each pumpkin plant to identify the male and the female flowers. One vine can have one or the other or both, but only the female flowers will turn into pumpkins.

Time was ticking. Ferréol stooped down to select a male pumpkin flower. In the middle of the flower was the stamen, the male reproductive organ of the flower, covered in **pollen.** Then he pinched a female flower, which has a sticky knob inside called the **stigma** that the pollen sticks to. Ferréol pressed the stigma of the female flower against the **anther** of the male flower, a process known as "the marriage." Within days buds appeared from underneath the female flowers. The pumpkins grew on the ground for four months until they were harvested.

THE FARMER and the VOLCANO

Ferréol explained to Edmond that if they could find the male and female parts of the vanilla plant, they could be pollinated and bear fruit on Réunion. Vanilla needs to grow in a region close to the equator, where the conditions are hot and humid, the soil is fertile and the nights are not too cold—like Mexico. Réunion's tropical climate was perfect. Formed from a volcanic hotspot in the Indian Ocean, the island is dominated by two volcanoes, one dormant (Piton des Neiges, or Snow Peak), and the other one of the world's most active (Piton de la Fournaise, or Peak of the Furnace).

PLANT SCIENCE

Joseph Henri Neumann was a French botanist and *horticulturalist* who worked at the Jardin des Plantes in Paris. Around 1830, he was the first botanist to research how to manually pollinate the vanilla plant. In 1837, Charles François Morren, a prominent botanist and a professor at the Botanical Spaces of the University of Liège in Belgium, used a blade of grass to attempt to hand-pollinate a vanilla orchid grown in a greenhouse. This failed attempt led botanists to think that the vanilla orchid couldn't produce fruit through hand-pollination.

VANILLA PLANTS TAKE ROOT

JUNE 26, 1819: Pierre Bernard Milius, the governor of Réunion, organized expeditions around the world to bring new species of plants to the island. Captain Pierre-Henri Philibert, commander of the vessels *Le Rhône* and *La Durance*, returned from an expedition to Guyana with *Vanilla pompona* cuttings. Though the plants grew on Réunion, they never bore fruit.

MAY 6, 1820: Commander Philibert and George Perrottet, a botanist, went to French Guiana, Java and the Philippines to collect vanilla cuttings for the governor. The *Vanilla tahitensis* they brought back did not survive on the island.

SEPTEMBER 25, 1822: A Monsieur Marchant arrived on Réunion with Mexican *Vanilla planifolia* cuttings from the Jardin des Plantes in Paris. These plants came from an earlier voyage to Mexico. This type of vanilla would eventually flourish on the island and bear fruit.

Young Edmond understood that these masses of ancient mountains, their slopes covered with rugged pathways, rich green forest and tilled farmland, could be the perfect place to grow vanilla. The plant needs shade and something for the vines to climb, as they grow to a height of up to 65 feet (20 meters). Vanilla is usually planted in a forest at the base of a tree so the **aerial roots** cling to the bark. It can also be planted between tall, thick stalks of sugarcane for shade, or even beside climbing poles in a plot of land covered by rows of sheer shade cloth. The Bellevue plantation had the perfect conditions. But still Ferréol's old orchid only flowered and never bore fruit.

A SCIENCE EXPERIMENT

Botany captivated Edmond. The science behind it seemed simple. While Ferréol met with the other plantation owners, Edmond searched through the pumpkin patch in search of bright-yellow pumpkin flowers. Methodically he analyzed each flower, differentiating male from female. He found a male and a female flower and pressed their anther and stigma together. With a handful of stones, Edmond marked the spot of his first science experiment. Later, in a letter to a journal, Ferréol wrote, "What Edmond lacked in schooling he made up for by his experience. He had been helping me in the garden for many years, and had seen me fertilizing other plants."

Edmond was a quick study. His first attempt at hand-pollination worked. As more pumpkins appeared, Ferréol believed it was the bees at work. But it was really Edmond. He was a botanist, a horticulturist—a scientist! In the months to come, young Edmond would solve that 300-year-old problem of getting the vanilla orchid to bear fruit.

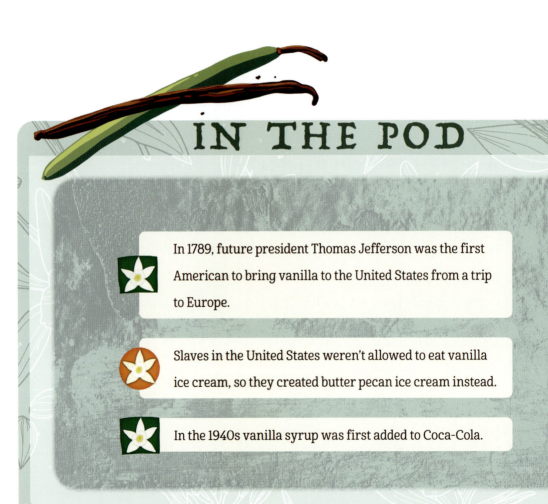

IN THE POD

- In 1789, future president Thomas Jefferson was the first American to bring vanilla to the United States from a trip to Europe.

- Slaves in the United States weren't allowed to eat vanilla ice cream, so they created butter pecan ice cream instead.

- In the 1940s vanilla syrup was first added to Coca-Cola.

NO MORE SUGAR

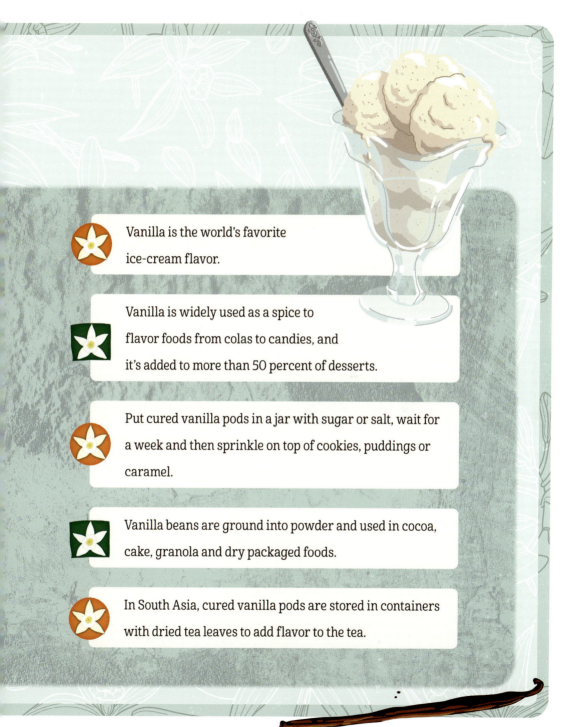

- Vanilla is the world's favorite ice-cream flavor.

- Vanilla is widely used as a spice to flavor foods from colas to candies, and it's added to more than 50 percent of desserts.

- Put cured vanilla pods in a jar with sugar or salt, wait for a week and then sprinkle on top of cookies, puddings or caramel.

- Vanilla beans are ground into powder and used in cocoa, cake, granola and dry packaged foods.

- In South Asia, cured vanilla pods are stored in containers with dried tea leaves to add flavor to the tea.

In 1427 the Aztecs conquered the Totonacs and discovered *xocolatl*, an early form of chocolate. The Totonacs made a beverage of crushed cocoa beans mixed with water and vanilla for flavoring. The vanilla pods were also used in medicines. This new treasure of war was more precious than gold. And it was delicious!

A NEW FLAVOR

Years later, in 1520, the Spanish conquistador Hernán Cortés fought against the Aztec emperor Montezuma, and he too discovered this special hot chocolate. Legend has it that Montezuma gave Cortés xocolatl in a gold cup. The emperor called it a divine drink that gave him strength when he was tired. Cortés returned to Spain with gold, silver, colorful gemstones and even a team of Aztec ball-playing athletes. But of all the treasures he had stolen, the most prized was the long dark-brown vanilla pods filled with thousands of tiny, oily black seeds. The Aztecs called vanilla **tlilxochitl**, or black pod, because of the color of the fruit when it was ready to use.

Soon the whole world wanted vanilla—kings, queens and royal physicians. Vanilla essence came to symbolize royalty. It became a main ingredient for pastry chefs. It was used in alcohol and tobacco, and pharmacists used it to remove the bitter taste in medicine. Vanilla became the world's favorite ice-cream flavor. But vanilla wasn't easy to get. It took time and money for ships to travel across the seas from Mexico to Europe and Asia. Vanilla production around the world needed to change, and Edmond would help make that happen.

VANILLA PRODUCTION IN MEXICO

1400s: The Mexican Totonacs use vanilla for medicine and rituals. They believe it is a sacred plant and continue to protect it today.

1571: Vanilla is added to the botany dictionary.

1650: Vanilla plantations are established throughout Veracruz, Mexico.

1800: Mexico is the only producer of vanilla. The country exports the vanilla bean all over the world until the mid-1800s.

1820s: The French arrive in Mexico and return to Réunion, France and Mauritius with cuttings in hopes of producing vanilla beans.

1910: The Mexican Revolution starts and there are wars throughout the country. Eventually the wars destroy most of the vanilla plantations.

1914: Vanilla farms are all shut down as a result of World War I. Mexico never regains its position as world supplier of vanilla.

1932: Oil is discovered in Poza Rica, which is the same region in Mexico where vanilla is grown. Oil is more valuable than vanilla or agriculture, so the land is cleared. This is called deforestation. The roots of the vanilla plant no longer have trees to climb, and this changes the entire agricultural environment. Vanilla production on a large scale stops.

1960: With more gas lines running through Mexico, there is even more deforestation. The use of artificial vanilla flavoring or *vanillin* increases.

1980-PRESENT: Production of vanilla in Mexico drops, making the country the third-largest producer in the world after Madagascar and Indonesia, a position that has not changed.

BEES *in* TREES

Ferréol always believed that one day vanilla would be Réunion's new agricultural product. But until that day came, the island had to rely on other produce. So early one spring morning, Ferréol and Edmond went to the garden to begin the ***caprification*** of the fig trees. Inedible male figs, called caprifigs, produce pollen. But to get that pollen to the female figs they need the fig wasp. Female fig wasps lay their eggs in caprifigs. When pollen-covered male wasps come out of the caprifigs, they transfer pollen to the edible-fig trees.

With a long wooden stick that had wire wrapped around its top, Ferréol picked some wild caprifigs and inserted a wire through each one, linking about eight of them on each wire. Once that was done, he pierced small holes in each caprifig. When he was finished, he had about seven strings. One by one, Edmond tossed them into the edible-fig trees. For the next few days, Ferréol and Edmond continued to make their wired pollinators to produce more edible figs. Ferréol's garden was one big science experiment.

NO FLOWERS *in the* GARDEN

In late December, in the spring of 1840 (spring in the southern hemisphere is from September to December), the time to pollinate Ferréol's old vanilla plant had passed. There would be no more clusters of white flowers on the vine. Ferréol inspected his fruitless vine. The wasps from the fig tree hadn't pollinated

the orchid as he had hoped, and he still couldn't figure out how to hand-pollinate the plant himself. As a botanist he knew that during the pollination season the vanilla flower blossoms at sunrise, folds by late morning, fades by noon and falls to the ground by sunset. Nature is perfectly timed. Ferréol would have to wait another year to see if the plant would flower and maybe bear fruit. The yellowish-white vanilla orchid produces flowers from September to December. If it's pollinated, the plants need eight to nine months to grow before the beans can be harvested. Nature needs that time to perfect the flavor and aroma.

A NEW TREASURE

Ferréol was exasperated that his experiment wasn't working. He wasn't alone—no other botanist or scientist had successfully hand-pollinated a vanilla orchid. Edmond saw Ferréol's frustration and wanted to help his master. Botanists study plant life, so Edmond knew he needed to start by comparing all the species of plants in Ferréol's garden. Were the flowers of the plants the same? How were they different? Which one was the male? Which one was the female?

Was the vanilla orchid like the pumpkin, which had both male and female flowers on the same vine? Did orchids need help from wasps, like figs did? So many questions needed answers. Edmond studied, analyzed and observed every microscopic detail. Science is research. Science is collecting data.

Edmond knew bees had it all figured out, and they made the science look simple as they buzzed from purple flowers to fig trees, replenishing and repopulating the earth one ***petal*** at a time.

VARIETIES of VANILLA

Vanilla planifolia: This edible orchid, native to Mexico, also grows in Madagascar and other islands in the Indian Ocean, including Réunion. The vanilla grown here is known as Bourbon vanilla. When it's in bloom, it has 10 to 15 clusters of white flowers on a vine. This vanilla has a mild fragrance, and its flower wilts by the end of the day. The roots are underground and external, so they cling to the bark to climb up a tree or pole. The fruit produced is called a pod, and it is long, light green and firm. It looks like a string bean. *V. Planifolia* has the most *vanillin*. Its flavor, which is sweet, rich, slightly floral, with subtle woody undertones, makes it a worldwide favorite.

Vanilla tahitensis: Named after the Tahiti islands, this edible bean has zigzag stems that are shorter and wider than that of *V. planifolia*. The flavor is produced quickly because the bean dissolves fast when heated. It is used in perfumes and in refrigerated and frozen foods.

Vanilla pompona: This long, plump bean nicknamed "banana vanilla" originates from Central America. This bean is mostly used for perfume because its aroma is floral, fruity and sweet.

A NEW TREASURE

THE ANSWERS WERE *in the* GARDEN

In order to help Ferréol, Edmond relied on the scientific process. Once again, Edmond searched through the garden for blossoming sweet potatoes, peppers, pumpkins and squash. He gently lifted the tiny purple, white or yellow-orange flowers. Edmond found the male, then the female part of each flower and pressed them together. He marked each plant that he had pollinated with a pebble. Within days, orange, green and yellowish buds burst from the thick green vines. This was it! With the appearance

of the small buds, there was no doubt that Edmond now knew the difference between the male and female flowers and how to hand-pollinate them himself.

Months later rows of pumpkins, squash, peppers, sweet yellow pineapples, dark pink cloves and bundles of brèdes (leafy greens) were ripe and ready to be harvested. The few slaves who remained at the plantation were busy working in the fields. Their hands were full and their baskets overflowed with ripe crops.

No one realized what Edmond was doing. Because he always played in the garden, everyone had ignored him as he ran back and forth, comparing all the plants and trees. But Edmond had succeeded in pollinating many of the vegetables in the garden, and he understood how the fig trees needed fig wasps. So far, though, he hadn't succeeded with the vanilla orchid. Edmond decided he had to go inside the orchid like a bee would. The male and female parts *must* be hidden inside, just like they were in the fig. And somewhere inside the one vanilla flower were both the male and female parts that had to be rubbed together in order to produce vanilla pods. Edmond concluded that the orchid must be different from all the other plants in the garden. He believed his research would change the world.

A NEW TREASURE

IN THE POD

- The smell of vanilla helps calm the brain and acts like a sedative, so it's been used as a treatment for depression, stress and anxiety.

- Vanilla pods contain small amounts of vitamins like niacin, vitamin B6, thiamine and riboflavin, all of which help the body function.

- A little vanilla and warm water helps with a cold.

It was 1841, and Edmond was 12 years old. He was now a young botanist and a farmer, who had learned Ferréol's techniques of hand-pollination and caprification. He knew that some plants needed other pollinators and that some could be hand-pollinated. He knew the vanilla plant was **hermaphroditic**—that it had both male and female parts. But how would he find them?

A WILTED FLOWER

Early one spring morning, Edmond examined Ferréol's Mexican vanilla plant. The old orchid vine had a few clusters of 10 to 15 white flowers, but only one or two opened each day. Edmond grabbed the one and only flower open that day. Where was the male part? Where was the female? The plant had to be examined. Edmond sat on the ground, grabbed one of his tiny bamboo twigs and held the flower up to his eyes to take a close look. There wasn't much time, as the flower would wilt by noon.

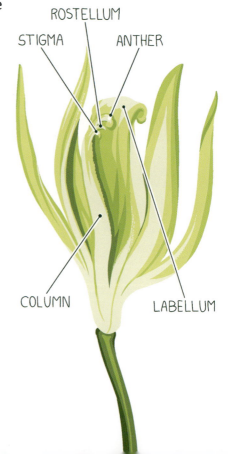

LE GESTE D'EDMOND

Step 1: The delicate white flower had to be destroyed. This was the only way to find the male and female reproductive parts. He had to be careful, as there wouldn't be another flower until the next morning. Edmond ripped open the middle of the flower. The petals were a little crushed, but they remained intact.

Step 2:  Using his bamboo twig, he gently moved the petals of the flower around. Edmond lifted up the bottom petal of the flower, known as the **labellum**, to see what was inside the flower. He knew he needed to find the pollen, just like bees do.

Step 3:  Edmond had to find the **column**, the fleshy part in the center of the flower that contains the male and female reproductive organs. He moved the bamboo twig around carefully and saw a thin membrane shaped like a flap. Edmond had just discovered the plant's **rostellum**. It's what separates the male part of the plant from the female.

Step 4:  With the bamboo twig, he gently lifted the rostellum. There was the male organ. It was kind of sticky. This was the *anther* of the *stamen*, the part of a flower where the pollen is produced. With the tip of the bamboo twig, he guided the anther to the female part of the plant, called the *stigma*, and pressed the two parts together. Just like the bees! Edmond had successfully hand-pollinated the vanilla plant for the first time in history.

Step 5: The bruised white petals were barely attached to the flower. If plants aren't pollinated, the flower becomes slightly yellow and limp and falls off. But Edmond was sure he had found the male and the female parts of the flower. Now he had to wait. But for how long? He hoped the orchid would bud the next day, just as the pumpkin had. But as a farmer, he knew it could take weeks.

24 HOURS LATER

The next day Edmond went to the garden and noticed the vanilla plant had begun to swell underneath the labellum. In the days that followed, Edmond analyzed his work. For years he had studied the changes in the plant life in the garden, so he knew that once a plant was fertilized, there had to be a bud. When

Edmond saw that the plant from the previous day had begun to bud, he hand-pollinated the only other flower on the vine. Step by step he repeated the same process.

The day after that, when Ferréol and Edmond were strolling through the garden, they saw two wilted flowers with two bold green vanilla buds forming underneath them. Ferréol stopped. He stared. He could not believe what he saw. Edmond told him what he'd done.

On the third morning, when the buds continued to swell and another flower appeared, Ferréol asked Edmond to show him the process. For the next few days Ferréol and Edmond repeated the process as new flowers opened and pods continued to appear. Edmond successfully hand-pollinated the orchid again and again. This was scientific evidence. Justice of the Peace Auguste Mézières-Lépervanche later wrote that his friend Ferréol was forced to face the facts once he saw Edmond repeat the same operation over and over again, achieving success every day.

RÉUNION'S NEW INDUSTRY

The community of Sainte-Suzanne soon learned of Edmond's discovery. The villagers, Ferréol's friends, plantation owners and their slaves all came to Bellevue to see the vanilla buds for themselves. They came to find out if the rumors they'd heard were true. Could a slave really have done this? This was a historic moment.

HOMEMADE VANILLA BEANS

1. Vanilla orchids mostly grow in the jungle, so they like a warm room with bright sunlight. Keep the room dark at night. The room temperature should be above 70 degrees F (21 degrees C). The bathroom is a good place to start your plant because of the humidity. The orchid cannot survive in cold weather, frost or winds.

2. You will need a pole or trellis for the vines to climb and the roots to cling to. As the plant grows, you will need to buy a larger pot and get a bigger trellis.

3. The soil should be kept moist so the roots do not get dry. Be sure to water every few days. In the spring and summer, the plant will need some fertilizer.

4. It will take three to four years before your plant will yield white flowers. Once the flowers appear, they must be hand-pollinated before they wilt. If pollination is done properly, buds will appear, and in nine months your vanilla pods will be ready to harvest.

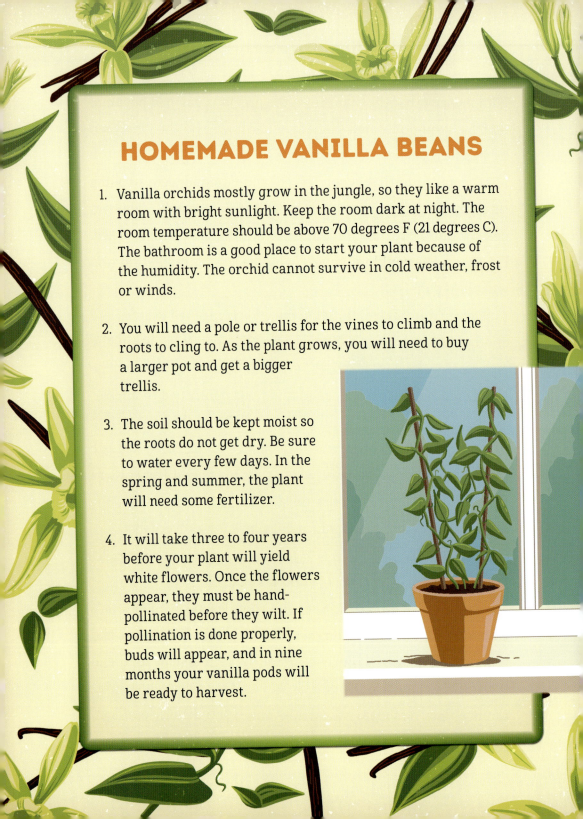

Ferréol wrote letters documenting the discovery and celebrating what would become Réunion's new industry. He wanted Edmond to receive credit for his work. "Walking with my faithful companion, I saw...a well-knotted pod," he wrote. "I was surprised, and pointed it out to him. He told me that it was he who had fertilized the flower. I refused to believe it, and passed by. But 2 or 3 days later I saw a second pod near the first. I then asked how he had done it. With the few flowers on the vine, he performed it in front of me, this operation that everyone practices today. The intelligent child had been able to discern, in the same flower, the male and female organs and put them in proper relation."

Ferréol sent those letters to the French Chambers of Agriculture, scientific journals and to Réunion's *Le Moniteur* newspaper to record Edmond's research. His process was given the name **le geste d'Edmond** (Edmond's gesture), and it was big news. Ferréol needed word of Edmond's discovery to reach people around the world. Ferréol wanted to make sure the world would never forget this "clever boy."

IN THE POD

People have been using vanilla as a medicine for centuries. Following are some of the benefits it's said to have.

 Vanilla has antibacterial properties and may help with acne and pimples.

 Vanilla is used in the cosmetics industry. It's added to perfumes, lipstick, soap, deodorants, lotions and hair-care products.

 A cured vanilla bean will stop skin from itching.

 Some people believe that cured vanilla beans can be used on the hair and scalp to promote hair growth.

 Some people believe that the beans can remove dark circles from under the eyes and tighten the skin.

News of Edmond's discovery spread from Saint-Suzanne to Madagascar, Seychelles, Tahiti, Indonesia, France and Mexico. Right away people said that it was impossible for a slave to have done this. When word reached France, Ferréol hoped the French government would honor and reward Edmond for his research. But the world was slow to acknowledge that young Edmond, a slave, had made the discovery.

VANILLA FARMING
Each vanilla plant must be *cultivated* so that hand-pollination can occur at the right time. The pod is handpicked after nine months. When it is ripe, the pod is green and has a canary or split tail—or as the French say, queue de serin. Each bean must then be handpicked from the pod. This takes a long time, and it's what makes vanilla production so expensive and labor-intensive, even today. If the pods are left on the vine too long, they will split and can no longer be used.

EDMOND'S CLASSROOM

Ferréol's scientific explanation of le geste d'Edmond in the *Le Moniteur* newspaper was too complicated for people to understand and left plantation owners confused. So the community gathered together again at Ferréol's plantation for a demonstration of the technique.

Once again Ferréol asked Edmond to hand-pollinate another orchid flower. Now the plantation owners needed to learn how

A CARRIAGE RIDE

to perform the hand-pollination process themselves. They asked Edmond to come to their farms, excited that Edmond would make them rich—he had just solved a 300-year-old mystery, using a 20-year-old vine. Ferréol welcomed their invitation. This gave Edmond the chance to travel comfortably, something he had never experienced before. It would be Edmond's first time leaving the Bellevue plantation.

TURN UP THE HEAT

In Mexico vanilla pods are placed in the hot sun for months to cure the beans. By 1851 David de Floris, the main vanilla producer in Saint-André, on Réunion Island, had found a way to mimic that kind of heat. He developed the "Réunionese process" with his neighbor, Ernest Loupy. It involves scalding the vanilla pods in hot water for several minutes, which keeps them from continuing to ripen, then wrapping them in woolen blankets and sealing them in crates. After 12 hours they turn brown in color and are ready to be removed from the crates and dried in the sun. The pods are then tied into bundles and packed into wooden boxes lined with a cloth that allows the beans to release their natural flavor, developing the characteristics that distinguish Bourbon vanilla (named after the island's former name). Vanilla farming is hard work!

FROM GLOBAL MARKETS *to* LOCAL GARDENS

Edmond and Ferréol began their expedition around Réunion in early spring of 1841 while the vanilla flowers were in bloom. Their custom horse-drawn coach left Sainte-Suzanne and trekked over wooden bridges to small villages and large plantations, navigating narrow, winding mountain roads. Edmond saw the shores of the Indian Ocean for the first time and the sails of the ships that docked in the harbor of the capital city, Saint-Denis.

There were about 140 plantations on the east coast of the island between Sainte-Suzanne and Saint-Philippe. Edmond was sent to Saint-André, Sainte-Marie, Saint-Benoît and other plantations around the island, including in his own community of Sainte-Suzanne. Their travels brought them to wealthy plantation owners such as David de Floris and to the Desbassayns plantations. At each stop Edmond taught the plantation owners, their family members and their slaves his hand-pollination technique. Even the owners of small plantations were eager to profit from the new vanilla industry. The journey took some time, as the vanilla plants at the plantations on the island were mostly grown in out-of-the-way places, such as in bamboo forests or shade houses.

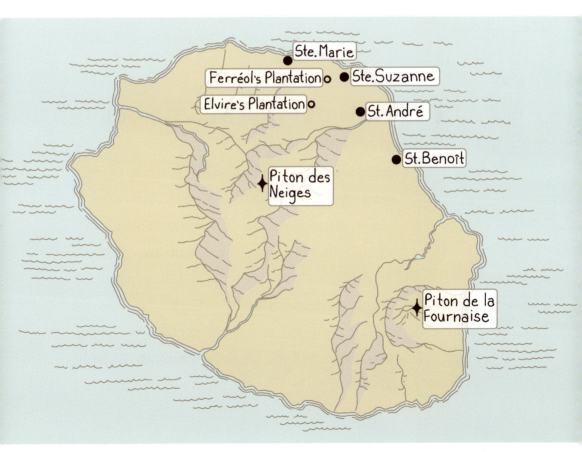

ANN RICHARDS

Between 1841 and 1847 Ferréol and Edmond created a new agricultural economy on Réunion—coffee and sugarcane were no longer the main products grown on the island. But it required patience, as it takes three to four years for vanilla plants to mature. Now parcels of land on the island had orchid vines planted around poles, covered by rows of sheer shade cloth, or the white flowers blossomed at the roots of trees in the bamboo forest. By 1847 the economy and environment of Réunion had changed. Yellow, white and green flowers blossomed everywhere.

THE MOST EXPENSIVE SPICE

The vanilla orchid must be tended to every day, which requires many laborers. This makes vanilla very expensive to produce. Thanks to the work of slaves, Réunion was on its way to producing more vanilla than Mexico, even though there were no bees on the island that could pollinate the orchid. Edmond had done what, until that time, people thought only the *Melipona* bee could do. Ferréol was convinced the whole world would soon be abuzz with the news. Edmond's discovery had

> **VANILLA TO VANILLIN**
> Vanillin is the primary component of the vanilla bean. French biochemist Nicolas-Theodore Gobley, in 1858, was the first to isolate pure vanillin crystals from the extracts of vanilla beans, determining vanillin to be the compound that gives vanilla its rich flavor and sweet taste. German chemists Ferdinand Tiemann and Wilhelm Haarmann did the same and succeeded in discovering the chemical structure of vanillin, which allowed them to make *synthetic* vanillin.

saved the economy, but there was still no recognition of his work.

In time, ships would no longer have to transport vanilla between Mexico and Europe. This would change the price of vanilla, as Mexico would no longer control the market. Edmond changed how food was distributed around the world, and his influence is still felt today.

THE SCIENTIFIC METHOD

At that time, it was hard to convince people that a slave could make such an important discovery. When word of Edmond's discovery reached

Tahiti, people there said that because Edmond hated his owner, he had destroyed the flower by stepping on it, which caused the pollination. Réunion plantation owners told their own tales. They said Edmond had been kissing a Creole girl and wanted to teach her about male and female parts, so he used the vanilla flower. Despite the rumors, Edmond's scientific research changed the world, and a scientist deserves credit. But that wasn't to happen.

IN THE POD

 The word *vanilla* is derived from the Spanish word *vainilla*, which means "little pod."

 Fresh vanilla beans have no smell or taste.

 Vanilla only grows in hot climates near the equator or in greenhouses.

 Vanilla must be cured in hot water and dried to create flavor.

 Bourbon vanilla from Réunion is considered a world favorite.

 Vanilla is the preferred scent for candles.

The French government had spent more than 20 years trying to start the vanilla industry on Réunion. The government had appointed explorers to bring vanilla orchid clippings from Mexico to the island because it had the perfect climate for growing the plant. But it wasn't until Edmond's discovery that those plans were finally realized. The colonizers knew it would take just a few years to establish a profitable industry on Réunion, but they needed slaves to cultivate and harvest the orchid—in other words, they needed free labor. That meant it wasn't in the French government's best interest for **slavery** to end. But the world was changing quickly. Many countries were bringing an end to slavery. For example, Britain abolished slavery in 1833, which meant colonies of the British empire had to follow suit. And many people in France were also against slavery.

SLAVERY IN CANADA
The first slave came to what is now known as Canada in 1628. He was a child who arrived in Quebec on a pirate ship from Madagascar. He was one of more than 4,000 slaves in Quebec, Ontario, Nova Scotia, Prince Edward Island and New Brunswick over the next 200 years. Slaves in Canada cleared forests and fields and built roads, highways and buildings. In 1743 Code Noir arrived from France as a guide to manage the slaves. The British parliament passed the Slavery Abolition Act on August 28, 1833, but the act didn't come into effect until August 1, 1834.

SOCIETY OF THE FRIENDS OF THE BLACKS

The Society of the Friends of the Blacks was formed in 1788 by Jacques-Pierre Brissot and Étienne Clavière to abolish the slave trade. They believed international support and cooperation were needed because the French colonizers were powerful. They modeled this organization after the Society for the Abolition of the Slave Trade, which their British friends Granville Sharp and Thomas Clarkson had founded a year earlier. Members of these organizations were attacked in the street for their beliefs and some were jailed for propaganda against the government.

EDMOND'S NEW NAME

The February **Revolution** of 1848 in France brought the July Monarchy under King Louis Philippe I to an end. A day before the formation of a new government made up of **abolitionists**, on April 28, 1848, a decree abolishing slavery in the French colonies was announced. The new government would begin the process of ending slavery, while continuing to bring indentured workers to the island. This news did not reach Réunion until a month later. The French declaration meant that the 64,700 slaves on the island—farm laborers, house servants, blacksmiths, overseers and **bossales**—would be free. The government on Réunion feared **emancipation** because there would be more freed men and women than colonizers. The French plantation owners didn't

like the change—it meant some of them would lose their land because they would now have to pay the freed slaves to harvest their crops.

Shortly after hearing the news, the Assembly of Property Owners from the north coast of the island met to discuss what the end of slavery would mean for their plantations. It was in their best interest to accept this fact, as they hoped it would help maintain social order, avoid a revolt and keep everyone working.

The time was right to make sure Edmond received credit and payment for his discovery. With pen in hand, Ferréol went to his

FÈT KAF CELEBRATION

desk and began a new letter-writing campaign to let the world know about Edmond's research. He enlisted the help of his friend Justice of the Peace Auguste Mézières-Lépervanche, and together they wrote to government officials and had articles published in newspapers and science publications. Ferréol was persistent.

Ferréol gave Edmond his freedom months ahead of the other slaves. It was time for Edmond to leave the plantation. The French declaration required that the names of all freed slaves in the colonies be added to the "civil list," or list of citizens, and to the county register in Sainte-Suzanne. That meant Edmond would also finally get a last name. In November 1848 he is listed

as "Citizen Edmon [sic], the son of deceased slaves Mélise and Pamphile." Around the world, it was common practice that slaves adopted the last name of their masters. Destined to be different, Edmond was given the last name Albius, from the Latin *albus/alba*, meaning "white"—like the vanilla orchid.

Though the world tried to ignore him, Ferréol made sure Edmond would never be forgotten. He had a **daguerreotype** taken of a young, handsome Edmond in a black jacket. It's one of the few images of Edmond that still exist today.

UNANSWERED LETTERS

Months after the new French government declared the end of slavery, the new governor of Réunion, Joseph Napoléon Sébastien Sarda-Garriga, announced that the Code Noir would no longer be used to manage the slaves.

Edmond had dreamed of leaving the plantation and going to the capital city to find work, just like many of his friends. He'd never forgotten the sound of the Indian Ocean or the sailing ships he'd seen as he'd traveled around the island, teaching the plantation owners how to hand-pollinate their vanilla plants. His dream was to become a cook on a large ship and travel the world, but he would need money to live, to buy food, clothes and shoes. There were no jobs in the small town of Sainte-Suzanne. While on the Bellevue plantation, Edmond had learned to cook and had also worked as a stonemason, cutting and preparing stones for buildings.

THE UNDERGROUND RAILROAD
Harriet Tubman was born around 1820. She was fearless. Harriet was nicknamed General Tubman because she actively helped hundreds of slaves escape the United States to Canada through the Underground Railroad, a network of routes and safe stopping places.

Ferréol wrote another letter to Sarda-Garriga, asking the French government to compensate Edmond for his contribution to the economy. Several weeks passed with no response. All of Ferréol's letters went unanswered. During this time the governor was traveling around the island, seeking to maintain the peace between the white plantation owners and the freed slaves. The French government's main concern was making sure the white plantation owners continued to make profits, as it was now harvest time. There was a lot of work to be done and money to be made from vanilla.

EMANCIPATION

On December 20, 1848, the process of implementing the abolition of slavery was finally finished. The freed men, women and children celebrated with a Fèt Kaf, a festival to mark the end of slavery that included singing, dancing and eating. "My friends, by decree of the French Republic…you are free," said Sarda-Garriga. "Liberty also means duties." He said that all freed men must have work contracts, and work was now compulsory. Those who didn't work would be punished. The notary and mayor of Saint-Denis, Candide Azéma, described the day as joyful for some and

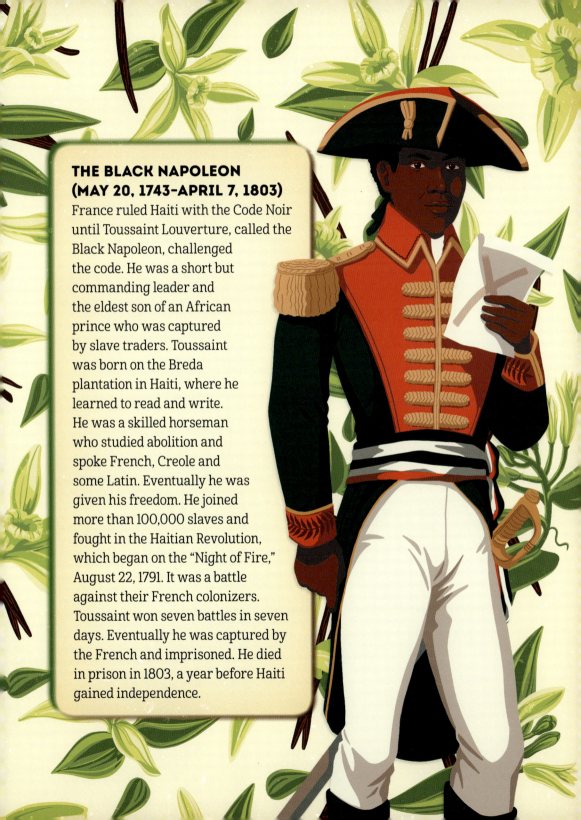

THE BLACK NAPOLEON
(MAY 20, 1743-APRIL 7, 1803)

France ruled Haiti with the Code Noir until Toussaint Louverture, called the Black Napoleon, challenged the code. He was a short but commanding leader and the eldest son of an African prince who was captured by slave traders. Toussaint was born on the Breda plantation in Haiti, where he learned to read and write. He was a skilled horseman who studied abolition and spoke French, Creole and some Latin. Eventually he was given his freedom. He joined more than 100,000 slaves and fought in the Haitian Revolution, which began on the "Night of Fire," August 22, 1791. It was a battle against their French colonizers. Toussaint won seven battles in seven days. Eventually he was captured by the French and imprisoned. He died in prison in 1803, a year before Haiti gained independence.

> **QUEEN NANNY AND THE CHRISTMAS REBELLION**
> In Jamaica, Queen Nanny, an escaped slave born to the Asante tribe in Ghana, led the Maroons, a group of formerly enslaved Africans, from 1728 to 1734. Nearly 100 years later, one of the largest slave revolts in Caribbean history began on December 25, 1831. The Christmas Rebellion, also known as the Baptist War, lasted for 11 days and involved more than 60,000 slaves rebelling against the British. On August 1, 1834, as in other British colonies, slavery was finally abolished in Jamaica.

sad for others. By the next day all the former slaves on Réunion had work contracts. The same day slavery ended, 500 indentured workers from India were brought to Réunion and were also given work contracts.

Knowing there was a pile of unanswered letters on the governor's desk, Ferréol could no longer wait on a response from the French government to compensate Edmond. He wasn't rich like the other plantation owners, but he gave Edmond some money and sent him off to the big city of Saint-Denis to chase his dreams. Edmond was no longer a slave—he was a free man. But in the end, the capital city would cost Edmond his freedom.

IN THE POD

- Vanilla farms are sometimes protected by armed guards.

- Vanilla beans are tattooed or marked so they can be identified by the farmer.

- Workers can hand-pollinate between 1,000 and 2,000 vanilla orchids in a day.

- It takes nine months for the vanilla seed pods to mature enough to harvest.

- Vanilla beans take three months to cure.

- Vanilla is still produced manually today with no machines. No chemicals or fertilizers are used.

January 1849 marked a new beginning for Edmond—a new year, a new life. He would no longer walk the stony paths of the plantation. Nineteen-year-old Edmond was living in the capital city of Saint-Denis, with its busy streets, tall buildings and modern architecture. It was a port for ships from around the world, and it was home to newspapers, the governor's mansion, the courthouse and the prison.

THE SHIP'S COOK

Evidence of the vanilla industry that he and Ferréol had started on the north coast of Réunion could be seen everywhere.

SHIPS AT SEA

The island's economy was thriving because of Edmond's discovery—that year the island exported more than 110 pounds (50 kilograms) of vanilla beans to France. As Edmond walked the city streets, rubbing shoulders with freed men, Creoles and rich and poor whites, he knew what he had accomplished. But with no recognition of his scientific work, he began to lose hope of receiving any payment from the French government. Still, he was determined to follow his dream of becoming a ship's cook, and he continued to walk the docks, looking for work on a ship. He never found it, and in the end Edmond had to settle in Saint-Denis, where he eventually found a job as a laborer.

THE END *of a* DREAM

In April 1851 he was hired as a cook and domestic servant in the home of an officer in the Saint-Denis **garrison**, Captain Joseph Mathurin Marchand. The job paid US $18 per week along with 20 cups of rice.

While Edmond was working there, some items went missing from Captain Marchand's home. He accused Edmond of stealing them. Edmond was arrested and held in the Saint-Denis prison. In the end, Edmond admitted to stealing a wallet, a pair of silver bracelets from a Chinese casket, a silver chain and a rosewood box of seashells, saying that he had been influenced by other people working in the home. But even more items disappeared. Edmond tried to say that those people might have taken these other items, but no one believed him. No one listened to the former slave. With Edmond's confession, the deputy prosecutor recommended he be tried by the Court of Assizes in Saint-Denis. In January 1852, Edmond Albius, age 23, was found guilty of theft and sentenced to prison for five years with hard labor. He had to pay the cost of the trial too.

SHACKLES *and* CHAINS

Edmond began his prison sentence. In the official documents he is described as 5 feet 6 inches (168 centimeters) tall with a round face, protruding forehead, black eyebrows, black eyes, black hair, thick lips, no beard and a round chin. The Saint-Denis prison

conditions were brutal. There was no clean water, and the mattresses were so dirty that many inmates chose to sleep on the floor. Some prisoners, including Edmond, wore a nine-pound (four-kilogram) iron collar that was chained to the wall, and others had an iron ball and chain shackled to their bare feet. The bossales, migrant laborers and indentured workers faced the harshest penalties of anyone in the prison. They were separated and treated

differently than white prisoners. The prison system essentially maintained the rules of Code Noir.

This new world was nothing like what Edmond had dreamed of. Word of his arrest reached the small village of Sainte-Suzanne after the trial. Ferréol knew that if former governor Sarda-Garriga had answered Ferréol's letters and recognized Edmond's contributions, Edmond would not have stolen from his employer. Instead the French government wanted to make an example out of the newly freed slave. Ferréol decided it was time to contact the French government again and ask for Edmond's freedom, along with financial **reparations** and recognition for his scientific research.

AN OPPORTUNITY

Réunion was exporting more and more vanilla every year, and it was thanks to Ferréol and Edmond. When slavery ended, the new government had created the Settlers' Compensation Act and formed the Colonial Bank for the plantation owners. They were compensated because they'd had to give contracts to the indentured workers, as some slaves had left and gotten other contracts elsewhere. The slaves received no reparations, financial or otherwise, for their past work. At the same time, Edmond's research was not documented in the history books, so his prison sentence was the perfect time for someone else to take credit for his discovery—someone who was also a botanist.

TONS OF VANILLA
A Timeline of Réunion's Vanilla Exports

1848: 50 pods

1867: 44,092 pounds (20,000 kilograms)

1880: 164,289 pounds (74,520 kilograms)

1885: 467,380 pounds (212,000 kilograms)

1891: 440,924 pounds (200,000 kilograms)

1898: 361,558 pounds (164,000 kilograms)

1899: 189,597 pounds (86,000 kilograms)

1900: 361,558 pounds (164,000 kilograms)

1930s: Disease, low prices and a drop in sales affect the vanilla market. Most of the farms stop producing the crop. Madagascar then becomes the world producer of vanilla.

THE WRITING DESK

It was difficult for Ferréol to see Edmond in prison. The kind young man was now in shackles and suffering in a cold, dirty prison. In 1852 Ferréol's friend Mézières-Lépervanche, the local justice of the peace, wrote a letter to Governor Louis Isaac Pierre Hilaire Doret. "I am writing to request grace for this unfortunate and interesting young man, as well as public remuneration in exchange for his discovery," he wrote. "If the government had granted him the reward that would have sheltered him from need, he would not have turned to crime to satisfy the tastes he

acquired when working for his former master." Ferréol wrote a letter to the public prosecutor to ask that Edmond's sentence be lightened. Even with the support of Sainte-Suzanne's justice of the peace, there was no response. But Ferréol didn't give up hope.

THE FIRST CREOLE

In 1852 Louis Henri Hubert Delisle became the first Creole governor of Réunion. Ferréol thought that Delisle must have read the articles about Edmond's discovery in Réunion's *Le Moniteur*

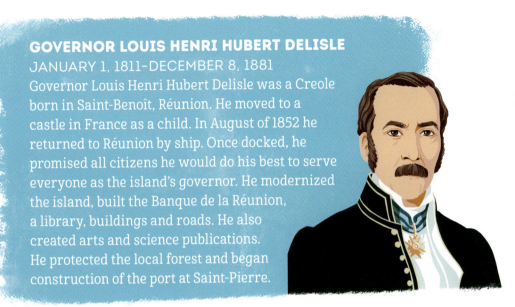

GOVERNOR LOUIS HENRI HUBERT DELISLE
JANUARY 1, 1811–DECEMBER 8, 1881
Governor Louis Henri Hubert Delisle was a Creole born in Saint-Benoît, Réunion. He moved to a castle in France as a child. In August of 1852 he returned to Réunion by ship. Once docked, he promised all citizens he would do his best to serve everyone as the island's governor. He modernized the island, built the Banque de la Réunion, a library, buildings and roads. He also created arts and science publications. He protected the local forest and began construction of the port at Saint-Pierre.

newspaper or heard of his journey in a horse-drawn carriage to the Desbassayns plantation in Saint-Paul or the David de Floris farm in Saint-André. Surely he would help Edmond.

In 1855 Ferréol wrote to Delisle. He asked the governor to show compassion for Edmond. He pointed out that Edmond was a model prisoner who had suffered in silence. He explained that with the sudden announcement of emancipation, Edmond, like other slaves, was not financially prepared. He'd been taken advantage of because of his youth and inexperience, and this is what had led him to steal. If anyone had a right to clemency, recognition and financial reward, Ferréol wrote, it was Edmond. It was entirely because of him that Réunion had a piece of the vanilla industry and that

people had come from everywhere to the island to learn of Edmond's technique.

THE PLANTATION HOUSE

Governor Delisle agreed! Edmond Albius was released in 1855, after serving three years in the Saint-Denis prison. Edmond returned to the protection of the Bellevue plantation to farm a plot of land that Ferréol gifted him. Edmond settled back into life on the plantation and worked as a farmer, stonemason and cook for several years. But the twists and turns of his story did not end there. Not long after he was released, another article was published claiming that Edmond was ungrateful, that he'd forgotten all the good things his master had done for him when he went to the city and that he'd ended up in bad company. Despite the story, Ferréol was as determined as ever to get Edmond's name into the history books.

From 1852 to 1860 Réunion produced and exported over 2,204 pounds (999 kilograms) of vanilla. The vanilla industry was profitable. But while the island prospered, Edmond remained poor and ignored. In 1860 Ferréol embarked on his final letter-writing campaign for Edmond. He sent letters to as many local officials as he could. Then, in 1861, Sainte-Suzanne's new justice of the peace, Monsieur Ganne, finally responded to his letter and asked for details about Edmond's research into pollinating the vanilla orchid. Ferréol replied and credited Edmond with the scientific discovery. "In this plant [pumpkin], the male and female flowers occur on different plants, and I taught the little black boy, Edmond, how to marry the male and female parts together," he wrote. "This clever boy had realized that the vanilla flower also had male and female elements, and worked out for himself how to join them together."

BETRAYED

In 1861, Mézières-Lépervanche sent a letter about Edmond's discovery to Eugène Volsy Focard, a chief judge of the Superior Court, who also managed the *Bulletin de la Société des sciences et arts de l'île de la Réunion*. The *Bulletin* was founded by Governor Delisle, who had freed Edmond. The next year, in 1862, Ferréol wrote a letter to the *Bulletin* to validate Edmond's research. Volsy Focard, who had also tried to help Edmond, replied that he too agreed with Ferréol. The letter-writing campaign would not have been successful without the help of Mézières-Lépervanche. As a justice of the peace, his letters lent credibility to Ferréol's description of how Edmond had solved the problem of hand-pollinating the vanilla plant.

It was time to add Edmond's name to Réunion's history books. Edmond's findings would finally be published in the *Bulletin*. Volsy Focard's article was titled "A Note on the Introduction and Fertilization of the Vanilla Plant on Bourbon Island," which made Edmond famous. In 1863 a copy of the article was given to Ferréol.

But Volsy Focard had a secret. Another botanist was trying to claim he had come up with the idea of hand-pollinating vanilla and had tried to take credit for Edmond's research while he was in prison. Volsy Focard would do everything he could to make sure that credit went to Edmond.

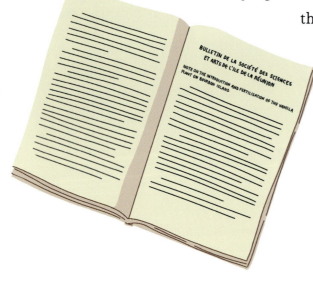

IN THE POD

 Vanilla has many industrial uses and is used to conceal the smell of rubber tires, paints and household cleaning products.

 Vanillin is added to cough medicine to eliminate the bitter taste and because vanilla is good for a sore throat.

 The pharmaceutical industry adds vanillin to medications because it helps with arthritis and allergies.

 Vanilla or vanillin is used to manufacture air fresheners.

 Scented wipes contain vanillin.

 Today 97 percent of vanilla flavor or fragrance used around the world is synthetic.

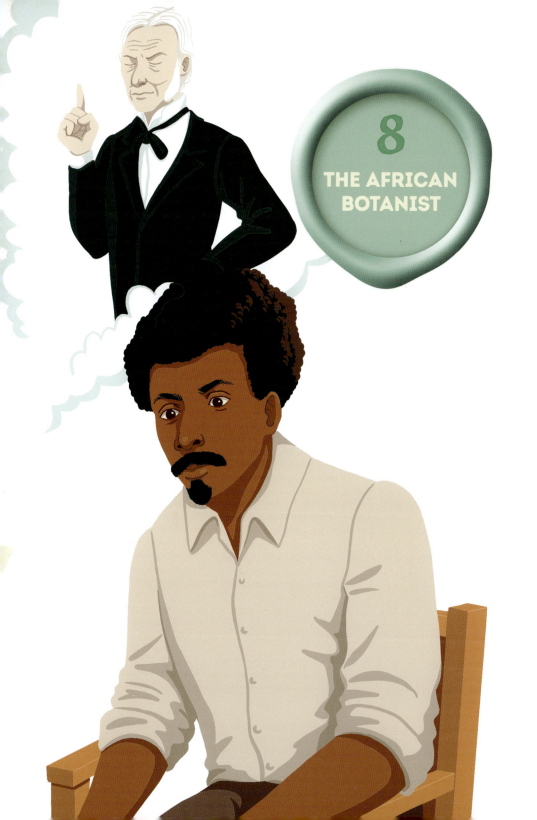

Ferréol had Volsy Focard's letter in his hand. It was unbelievable! A prominent botanist named Jean Michel Claude Richard claimed to have discovered the hand-pollination technique in 1837, while in Paris. In the following year, he said, he had visited Réunion and taught the plantation owners manual pollination while eight-year-old Edmond secretly watched.

This was a blatant act of betrayal—Richard and Ferréol were colleagues, friends! Richard had studied orchids but had made no such discovery. He had tried to figure out how to pollinate the vanilla orchid, but like other botanists of the time, he had failed.

NO RESEARCH, NO DATA

Ferréol's words were sharp. "No one could possibly believe that I would be stupid enough or audacious enough to try to pass off [Richard's] discovery as something new," he wrote. "Mr. Richard's memory is playing tricks on him…[he] imagines that he taught the technique to the person who discovered it! Let us leave him to his fantasies." Like people around the world, from France to Tahiti and even some on Réunion, Richard believed that an uneducated slave did not have the ability to make such an important discovery. Not so, replied Ferréol. "What Edmond lacked in schooling he made up in experience," he wrote back to Volsy Focard. "He had been helping me in the garden for many years and seen me fertilizing other plants." Richard could provide no evidence that he had made any such discovery.

Ferréol then read to Edmond the letters he had exchanged with Volsy Focard and the article the judge had written. He wanted Edmond to understand that his research would soon be validated. Finally, after more than 20 years, Edmond would be formally recognized for creating the vanilla industry on Réunion, and doubters around the world would be silenced. At this time Ferréol was not well and was unable to travel. They agreed that Edmond would deliver Ferréol's letter to Volsy Focard. While there, Edmond would give a demonstration of hand-pollination to set the record straight. And artist Antoine Louis Roussin, another founding member of the *Bulletin*, would paint Edmond's portrait.

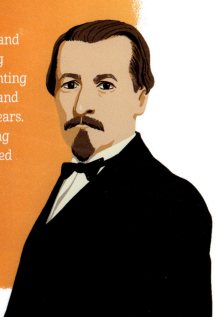

ANTOINE LOUIS ROUSSIN
MARCH 3, 1819–SEPTEMBER 18, 1894
Antoine Louis Roussin was born in France and then moved to Réunion. He set up a painting studio, and when he found an old offset printing press for doing **lithography**, he repaired it and produced more than 400 images over 40 years. He worked as a painter, high-school drawing teacher and photographer. His work included portraits of officials, famous people, public monuments and the island's animals and flowers. Roussin published over 200 articles about Réunion and he co-founded the Society of Sciences and Arts of Réunion Island.

A HISTORY LESSON

In 1863 Superior Court judge and historian Eugène Volsy Focard published an article on the history of vanilla and Edmond's contribution. It was called "Le vanillier, la vanilla" (The vanilla plant and vanilla). Beside the story was an image of Antoine's portrait of Edmond Albius, age 34, holding a single vanilla vine. Edmond had made history!

It is because of the support of Ferréol, Mézières-Lépervanche, Volsy Focard and Roussin that the history of vanilla is documented. At that time Réunion's vanilla industry was on its way to producing more beans than Mexico. The white plantation owners became rich. Volsy Focard sent a letter to the vanilla growers on the island requesting a financial "gesture of recognition" for Edmond. He wrote, "Let's ask them for a reward for the person who, each day, contributes to their wealth." Roussin asked the local agricultural community to help Edmond by giving him a few bundles of vanilla, a house with a straw roof and some land to work as payment. Sadly, there was no response.

AFRICAN ART

Roussin gave Edmond signed copies of his portrait and the story to give to his soon-to-be wife Marie-Pauline Bassana, his family and friends. Once again Edmond was celebrated on the Bellevue plantation. Ferréol wrote a note to Roussin on behalf of Edmond and thanked him for his support. History recorded Edmond as the inventor of the hand-pollination technique that came to be known as "le geste d'Edmond" (Edmond's gesture). The legends, the rumors and the debates about his discovery were finally put to rest.

A WEDDING and a FUNERAL

In 1871, at age 42, Edmond married Marie-Pauline, a seamstress and farmer. The wedding was held in Sainte-Suzanne. Her father, Paranton Bassana, was the chief sugar producer at a local factory. His position gave him elite status because his salary was four times that of other workers. Because of her father's success, Marie-Pauline owned property in Commune Carron, a few miles

from Sainte-Suzanne. Edmond had a new home and was finally able to leave the Bellevue plantation.

The following year, in 1872, Ferréol died. At the time of Ferréol's death, Edmond's profession is recorded as farmer, stonemason and cook. For the next five years, Edmond and his wife lived in Commune Carron. They didn't have children. She died in 1876 and left her home and property to Edmond and her father.

Four years after the death of his wife, on August 9, 1880, Edmond died in the hospital in Sainte-Suzanne of unknown causes. He was 51. Edmond's obituary appeared in the *Le Moniteur* newspaper in the "faits divers," or "snippets," column. His obituary mentioned Volsy Focard's 1863 article and noted Roussin's pleas for a pension or reparations for Edmond. "The very man who, at great profit to this colony, discovered how to pollinate vanilla flowers has died in the public hospital at Sainte-Suzanne," the obituary said. "It was a destitute and miserable end."

A SIMPLE LIFE

Edmond's obituary was incorrect. Although Edmond never received financial reward for his discovery, he did achieve some measure of success in the end. He married and lived in his own home. The vanilla vine on Réunion's coat of arms bears witness to his success in creating a viable vanilla industry on the island.

JEAN MICHEL CLAUDE RICHARD
AUGUST 16, 1783–DECEMBER 27, 1868
Richard was a French botanist, landscaper and gardener in Senegal. In 1831 he brought thousands of new tropical plants to Réunion. He was appointed honorary director of the State Garden in Saint-Denis, and his portrait appears in the book *Album de l'île de la Réunion*. Stories describe Richard as an energetic botanist and an amusing storyteller, infamously known as the botanist who tried to take credit for inventing le geste d'Edmond.

A statue of Edmond holding a vanilla vine is erected at a bus stop in Sainte-Suzanne, near the Bellevue plantation, and Edmond Albius College is named in his honor. The hand-pollination technique developed by Edmond is still used today. Since 1848, the people of Réunion celebrate the abolition of slavery and the importance of freedom with the Fèt Kaf festival. Edmond Albius may have been born enslaved, but he became Réunion's most famous Creole.

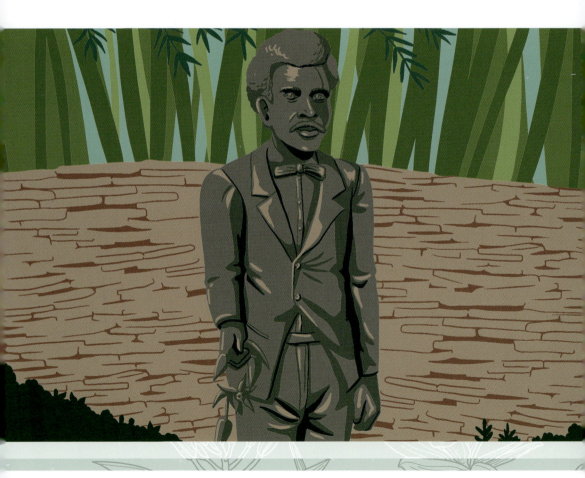

THE AFRICAN BOTANIST

IN THE POD

 About 80 percent of the world's vanilla is produced in Madagascar.

 Madagascar vanilla is called Madagascar Bourbon.

 There are two dry seasons each year in Madagascar, which occur a few months apart. This allows for propagation or cutting of the vanilla roots to produce more plants.

 In Madagascar, vanilla farmers sleep next to their crops to protect them from thieves.

 The current price of vanilla is as high as US$8 a pound ($17 a kilogram), but the farmers make less than $2 dollars per day.

TIME LINE

1819-1822: Vanilla plants arrive on Réunion Island.

1829: Edmond is born in Sainte-Suzanne to slaves Mélise and Pamphile.

1836: Botanist Charles Morren discovers the orchid cannot flower without the *Melipona* bee.

1841: Edmond develops a method of hand-pollination.

1848: Edmond is given his freedom, along with the surname Albius, and he leaves the Bellevue plantation for the capital city of Saint-Denis.

1851: Edmond is hired by Captain Joseph Mathurin Marchand as a cook and servant.

1851: Vanilla production booms on Réunion.

1852: Accused of theft by Captain Marchand, Edmond is sentenced to prison for five years with hard labor, and he must pay the cost of the trial.

1855: Edmond is granted early release from prison and returns to Ferréol's plantation.

1862: Volsy Focard publishes a story about Edmond's discovery in the *Bulletin of the Society of Sciences and Arts*.

1863: Focard publishes another story, this one with a lithograph of Edmond by Antoine Roussin.

1871: Edmond Albius, age 42, marries Marie-Pauline Bassana, a seamstress and farmer.

1872: Ferréol Bellier-Beaumont dies.

1876: Marie-Pauline Bassana dies.

1880: Edmond Albius dies.

GLOSSARY

abolitionists—people who wanted to stop, or abolish, slavery

aerial roots—roots that don't grow down but up into the air

anther—the pollen-producing part of the stamen (the male reproductive organ of a flower)

bossales—African-born slaves in a European colony

botanist—Scientists who study plants

botany—the scientific study of plants

caprification—a method of pollinating the edible fig tree by hanging caprifigs in its branches (caprifigs are figs that house fig wasps, which carry pollen to edible and inedible figs)

census—an official count of the number of people living in a country

Code Noir (Black Code)—a document containing 60 articles on how slave owners in the French colonies were to regulate the lives, purchase, punishments, religion and treatment of their slaves

coffles—groups of prisoners, enslaved people or animals that are chained or tied together in a line

colonizers—people who claim and take power over another country

column—a fleshy, finger-like structure in the center of the flower that contains the orchid's reproductive system

Creole—a person descended from French settlers and Malagasy slaves; also the language that has developed from a mixture of French, African, Indian and Malagasy (Madagascar) languages

cultivate—to prepare land for growing crops

daguerreotype—an early type of photograph produced on a silver or silver-covered copper plate

emancipation—the process of giving people social or political freedom and rights

enslaved—forced into slavery, becoming the property of someone else

ephemeral—lasting for a very short time, such as blooms on a flower that will wilt after a few hours

garrison—a military post or the place that houses the soldiers living in or defending a town or building

hermaphroditic—having both male and female parts

horticulturalist—a person whose work involves growing fruits, vegetables, flowers or ornamental plants

houseboy—a derogatory colonial term for a non-white young male domestic slave or servant

indentured workers—legally free people who are contracted to work without a salary for a specific length of time in exchange for eventual payment or debt repayment, which essentially amounted to forced labor

labellum—the lower-middle petal of the flower, which is larger than the other petals and often attracts pollinators

le geste d'Edmond—Edmond's gesture, referring to the specific technique of pollinating the vanilla orchid by lifting the rostellum

lithography—a printing process that involves using a stone or metal block on which an image has been drawn with a greasy medium that attracts oil-based ink

master—a person who employs a servant or owns a slave

Melipona—a genus of honeybees of tropical America that comprises small bees with a vestigial but functionless stinger

noirs de pioche—a term for male slaves who worked in the fields (the word *pioche* means "pickax")

overseers—people whose job it is to make certain that things are being done correctly

petal—one of the brightly colored parts that forms a flower. Orchids always have three petals. Two are normal, and the third is a highly specialized petal called a labellum (lip).

plantation—an agricultural estate, usually worked by slaves

pollen—a powder produced by the male part of a flower that causes the female part of the same type of flower to produce seeds. It is carried by insects or the wind, or can be transferred by hand.

reparations—amends for a wrong one has done, sometimes in the form of money

revolution—a radical change in the way a country is governed, usually involving a different political system and often using violence or war

rostellum—a thin membrane or flap that separates the male organ of an orchid from the female organ

slavery—the practice of owning other people and forcing them to work for and obey their owners

slaves—people who are legally owned by someone else and have to work for that person

stigma—the sticky area at the tip of the pistil, which receives pollen

still—a type of machine used to distill or make liquor such as rum

sugar press—a machine that crushes sugarcane to extract the juice

synthetic—made artificially rather than naturally

tlilxochitl—the name originally given to the vanilla plant by the Aztecs, meaning "black pod"

vanillin—the compound in vanilla beans that gives vanilla its distinct flavor and aroma. It can also be prepared synthetically.

xocolatl—a beverage of the Aztecs, made from ground cocoa beans and water and flavored with spices such as chilies or vanilla. It's considered by some people to be the earliest form of chocolate.

RESOURCES

Bourbon Vanilla: france.fr/en/article/all-you-need-to-know-about-bourbon-vanilla-in-just-5-minutes/

Edmond Albius: cbc.ca/radio/ideas/history-vanilla-slavery-jhi-lecture-eric-jennings-1.6964317

Edmond's Statue: portail-esclavage-reunion.fr/en/lieux-de-memoire/the-slave-mario-and-the-black-madonna/

Grow Your Own Vanilla: doityourself.com/stry/how-to-plant-and-grow-vanilla-beans

History of Mexican Vanilla: mexicanvanilla.com/pages/history-of-vanilla

History of Reunion: britannica.com/place/Reunion

History of Reunion Vanilla: en.reunion.fr/discover/gastronomy/fragrances-and-spices/discover-the-best-vanilla-in-the-world

Melipona Bee: beekeepclub.com/the-melipona-bee-a-stingless-honey-maker

SLAVERY in CANADA:

bccns.com/our-history

canada.ca/en/canadian-heritage/campaigns/black-history-month/historic-black-communities.html

fb.historicacanada.ca/education/english/black-history-in-canada/10

historymuseum.ca/virtual-museum-of-new-france/population/slavery

humanrights.ca/story/story-black-slavery-canadian-history

ontariohistoricalsociety.ca/wp-content/uploads/2020/06/slavery_in_canada.pdf

thecanadianencyclopedia.ca/en/timeline/black-history

SLAVERY in the UNITED STATES:

britannica.com/topic/African-American/Slavery-in-the-United-States

history.com/topics/black-history/slavery

jimcrowmuseum.ferris.edu/timeline/slavery.htm

Links to external resources are for personal and/or educational use only and are provided in good faith without any express or implied warranty. There is no guarantee given as to the accuracy or currency of any individual item. The author and publisher provide links as a service to readers. This does not imply any endorsement by the author or publisher of any of the content accessed through these links.

ACKNOWLEDGMENTS

To Mommy, thanks for your words…"yuh come far."

To my father, a great griot (storyteller), who wanted to write a book.

To my children: Talithia, my little girl, who continues to follow her dreams—keep going! And to Rashad, who's always on stage—the world is finally ready for you, superstar!

To my dearest George Knight: Friends make the best family members.

To all my friends and family: Thank you for your support always.

Special thanks to professor Stephen Rockel at the University of Toronto, a specialist in African history, for his historical review of this book.

To Orca Book Publishers: Thank you for believing in Edmond's story—a story that changed the world!

INDEX

abolitionists, 10, 58, 59, 93
aerial roots, 11, 21, 93
agriculture
 fertilization of plants, 18, 29, 38, 39
 plantations, 4, 9, 29, 94
Albius, Edmond
 aspirations, 15, 62–63, 66, 70–72
 as botanist, 16–17, 21–22, 38, 48–51
 credit for discovery, 78–80, 84–87
 early life, 2–6, 15–17, 38
 freedom granted, 60–62
 legacy, 87, 89–90
 le geste d'Edmond, 39, 44, 94
 marriage, 87–88, 89
 portrait of, 85, 87
 prison sentence, 72–74, 75–78
 return to Bellevue, 78–80
 timeline of events, 92
anther, 18, 39, 93
Aztecs, 26–27

banana vanilla (*Vanilla pompona*), 20, 32
Bassana, Marie-Pauline, 87–88, 92
bees
 Melipona, 7–8, 17
 and pollination, 6, 8
Bellevue plantation
 about, 2–5, 14–15
 life at, 5–6, 78
 See also Bellier-Beaumont, Ferréol
Bellier-Beaumont, Elvire, 2, 5
Bellier-Beaumont, Ferréol
 as botanist, 5–6, 29, 38

garden walks with Edmond, 5–6, 15–17
gifts to Edmond, 15, 61–62, 66, 78
hand-pollination efforts, 7–8, 29–31
letter-writing campaigns, 43–44, 60–64, 74, 75–78, 84–86
treatment of slaves, 4–5
Bellier-Beaumont plantation, 2, 14
Bonaparte Island, 8
bossales, 59, 73, 93
botanists, 5, 93
botany, 6, 93
Bourbon Island. *See* Réunion Island
Bourbon vanilla
 of Madagascar, 91
 scalding process, 50
 Vanilla planifolia, 17, 20, 32
 world-wide demand, 55
Britain
 abolishment of slavery, 58
 abolitionists, 59
British colonies, slave revolt, 66

Canada
 slavery in, 58
 Underground Railroad, 63
caprification, 29, 93
chocolate, 26–27
clove production, 9, 14, 34
Code Noir (Black Code)
 application of, 5, 9, 62, 74
 in Canada, 58
 defined, 4, 93
 in Haiti, 65
coffee production, 4, 9, 14, 52
coffles, 8, 93

colonizers
 attitude of masters, 3, 4–5, 9, 62
 defined, 93
 failure to reward Edmond, 86–87
 need for workforce, 52, 58, 66
 and slave rebellions, 10, 65, 66
 slave trade, 8, 10, 58–59
 use of work contracts, 64, 66, 74
 See also vanilla industry on Réunion Island
column, 39, 93
Cortés, Hernán, 26–27
cosmetics industry, 45
cotton production, 9
credit for discovery
 disbelief, 48, 53–54, 84
 effort to defame Edmond, 53–54, 78–79
 Ferréol's letters, 43–44, 60–64, 74, 75–78, 84–85
 lack of compensation, 66, 74
 publication of Edmond's discovery, 79–80
 supporters of Edmond, 75–76
Creole heritage, 5, 6, 76, 90, 93
Creole language, 16

daguerreotype, 62, 93
Delisle, Louis Henri Hubert, 76–78, 80
Desbassayns plantation, 10, 51, 77

Edmond. *See* Albius, Edmond
emancipation, 59, 64–66, 74, 93
enslaved, 2, 93

97

Ferréol. *See* Bellier-
  Beaumont, Ferréol
Fét Kaf festival, 64, 90
fig production, 29, 34
fig wasp, 29, 34
Floris, David de, 50, 51, 77
Focard, Eugène Volsy, 79,
  80, 86–87, 92
France
  abolitionists, 58, 59
  Revolution of 1848, 59
  slave revolt, 10, 65
  and slave trade, 8, 10, 59
  unfair laws, 2, 4–5, 58,
    64, 66
French government
  abolition of slavery, 59–62
  colonial independence,
    65
  failure to reward
    Edmond, 48, 66, 75
  makes example of
    Edmond, 74
  and vanilla industry, 58

Haiti, slave revolt, 65
hand-pollination
  and bees, 7–8, 17
  experiments, 7–8, 19,
    33–34
  figs, 29, 34
  to improve pollination,
    21–22, 33–34
  pumpkins, 17–18, 21–22,
    34
  vanilla flower
    technique, 29–31,
    38–41, 48–51
hermaphroditic, 38, 93
horticulturalist, 19, 93
houseboy, 2–5, 93

indentured workers, 10, 59,
  66, 73, 93
India, 8, 66

labellum, 39, 94
Le Code Noir (The Black
  Code)
  application of, 5, 9, 62, 74
  in Canada, 58
  defined, 4, 93
  in Haiti, 65
le geste d'Edmond, 39, 44,
  87, 94
Le Moniteur (newspaper),
  45, 48, 88–89
letter-writing campaigns
  and clemency for
    Edmond, 75–78
  and compensation,
    66, 74
  credit for discovery,
    84–85, 89
  Ferréol's letters, 43–44,
    60–64, 74, 75–76,
    84–86
  publication of
    Edmond's discovery,
    79–80
  support for Edmond,
    75–76, 86
lithography, 85, 94
Loupy, Ernest, 50
Louverture, Toussaint, 65

Madagascar, vanilla
  industry, 28, 32, 75, 91
Marchand, Joseph
  Mathurin, 72, 92
masters, 3, 4–5, 9, 62, 94
Maya people, 17
Melipona bee, 7–8, 17, 52, 94
Mexico
  vanilla industry, 28, 50,
    53, 86
  vanilla pollination, 7–8,
    17, 52
Mézières-Lépervanche,
  Auguste, 15, 41, 61,
  75–76, 79–80

Montezuma, 26–27
Morren, Charles François,
  7–8, 19, 92
Neumann, Joseph Henri,
  7–8, 19
noirs de pioche, 5, 94

orchid plant family, 10
overseers, 10, 94

perfumes, 32, 45
petals, orchid, 39, 94
plantations
  crops, 4, 9, 29, 33–34
  defined, 94
  slaves on, 2–5, 9, 14
pollen, 18, 94
pollination process
  and bees, 7–8, 17
  experiments, 7–8, 19,
    33–34
  fertilization of plants,
    18, 29, 38, 39
  figs, 29, 34
  pumpkins, 17–18, 21–22,
    34
  vanilla flower
    technique, 29–31,
    38–41, 48–51
pumpkin production,
  17–18, 21–22, 34

reparations, 74, 94
resources, 95
Réunion Island
  climate, 18–19, 21
  economy, 9, 14–15, 52,
    58, 74
  history of, 2–5, 8–10,
    14–15
  impact of emancipation,
    59–60, 62, 64, 66
  legacy of Edmond,
    89–90
  map, 51

Réunion Island (continued)
   Saint-Denis, 66, 70–74, 75
   timeline of events, 20
   See also vanilla industry on Réunion Island
revolutions, 8, 59, 94
Richard, Jean Michel Claude, 84–85, 89
rostellum, 39, 94
Roussin, Antoine Louis, 85, 86, 87
rum production, 14

Saint-Denis, 66, 70–74, 75
Sarda-Garriga, Joseph Napoléon Sébastien, 62, 64, 74
slave names, 2, 61–62
slavery
   abolition, 10, 58–62
   defined, 94
   slave trade, 8, 10, 59
slaves
   bossales, 59, 73, 93
   conditions of, 3–5, 8–10
   defined, 94
   emancipation, 59, 64–66, 74, 93
   noirs de pioche, 5, 94
   rebellions of, 10, 65, 66
   slave names, 2, 61–62
   unfair laws, 2, 4–5, 58, 64, 66
   as workforce, 48, 52, 58
Spanish conquistadors, 26–27

stigma, 18, 39, 94
still (liquor), 14, 94
sugarcane production
   and slaves, 4, 14
   and vanilla, 21, 52
sugar press, 14, 94
synthetic vanilla, 53, 81, 94

timeline of events
   life of Edmond, 92
   vanilla industry, 20, 28, 75
tlilxochitl, 27, 94

United States
   Underground Railroad, 63
   and vanilla, 22

vanilla
   and Aztecs, 26–27
   farming of, 55, 67, 91
   health benefits, 35, 45, 81
   organic, 67
   price of, 91
   synthetic, 53, 81, 94
   vanillin, 53, 81, 94
   world-wide demand, 10–11, 27, 53
vanilla flavoring, 22–23, 26–27, 32, 81
vanilla industry on Réunion Island
   demonstration of technique, 48–51
   failure to reward Edmond, 86–87

   growth of, 51, 52–53, 70–71, 79
   labor-intensive crop, 48, 52, 58, 67
   news of successful pollination, 41, 43–44
   scalding process, 50
   timeline of events, 20, 75
vanilla orchids
   aerial roots, 11, 21, 93
   growing conditions, 18–19, 21, 42
   grown at home, 42
   le geste d'Edmond, 39, 44, 87, 94
   pollination attempts, 7–8, 19, 38–41
   publication of Edmond's discovery, 79–80
   varieties, 20, 32
Vanilla planifolia, 17, 20, 32
vanilla pods
   scalding process, 50
   uses, 23
Vanilla pompona, 20, 32
vanilla powder, 23
vanilla production
   in Mexico, 28
   world-wide demand, 27
vanilla scent, 35, 55, 81
vanilla syrup, 22
Vanilla tahitensis, 20, 32
vanillin, 53, 81, 94

xocolatl, 26–27

ANN RICHARDS is a Jamaican Canadian writer from Brampton, Ontario, who has always wanted to write books about African history. She enjoys studying and writing about different cultures. One day she plans to visit Ghana's Elmina slave castle, known as the Door of No Return, to research more stories. Ann has written for the *London Free Press* and *Tekawennake News*. *The True Story of Vanilla: How Edmond Albius Made History* is Ann's debut book.

ARDEN TAYLOR is a Toronto-based freelance illustrator. A graduate of Sheridan College with an honors bachelor of illustration, she enjoys digitally creating colorful illustrations of architecture and people and designs for wallpaper and other projects. Her clients include *Hazlitt Magazine* and the California Institute of Technology, and her work has been featured in various magazines, newspapers, advertising campaigns and websites.